Apple Trees

by Gail Saunders-Smith

Pebble Books

an imprint of Capstone Press

Pebble Books

Pebble Books are published by Capstone Press
151 Good Counsel Drive, P.O. Box 669, Mankato, Minnesota 56002
http://www.capstone-press.com

2 3 4 5 6 07 06 05 04 03 02

Library of Congress Cataloging-in-Publication Data
Saunders-Smith, Gail.
    Apple tress / by Gail Saunders-Smith.
    p. cm.
    Includes bibliographical references (p. 23) and index.
    Summary: In simple text and photographs, describes an apple tree as it goes
through the seasons.
    ISBN 1-56065-490-2
    1. Apples—Juvenile literature. 2. Season—Juvenile literature. [1. Apples.
2. Seasons.] I. Title.
SB363.S28 1997
634'.11—dc21   97-23593
                                                                          CIP
                                                                           AC

Editorial Credits
Lois Wallentine, editor; Timothy Halldin and James Franklin, designers;
Michelle L. Norstad, photo researcher

Photo Credits
Michelle Coughlan, 6
Winston Fraser, 8
Dwight Kuhn, cover, 16
John Marshall Outdoor Photography, 1, 18
Mark Turner, 10, 14
Unicorn Stock / Jim Shippee, 4; Martha McBride, 3, 20
Valan Photos / J.A. Wilkinson, 3, 12

Table of Contents

In winter, apple trees
have no leaves.

In spring, apple trees
have some leaves.

8

In spring, apple trees
have many blossoms.

10

In summer, apple trees
have no blossoms.

In summer, apple trees
have some apples.

In summer, apple trees
have many leaves.

16

In fall, apple trees
have many leaves.

18

In fall, apple trees
have many apples.

In fall, apple trees have ripe apples. The apples are ready to pick.

Words to Know

blossom—a flower on a fruit tree or other plant

fall—the season between summer and winter; the weather becomes cooler.

spring—the season between winter and summer; the weather becomes warmer and plants begin to grow.

summer—the season between spring and fall; the weather is at its warmest.

winter—the season between fall and spring; the weather is at its coldest.

Read More

Burckhardt, Ann L. *Apples.* Mankato, Minn.: Bridgestone Books, 1996.

Davies, Kay and Wendy Oldfield. *My Apple.* First Step Science. Milwaukee: Gareth Stevens Publishing, 1994.

Internet Sites

All About Apples
http://www.lecrunch.ie/about.html

Apples & More
http://www.urbanext.uiuc.edu/apples

Just for Kids
http://www.bestapples.com/new/kids

Note to Parents and Teachers

This book describes and illustrates apple trees in each season. The text repeats to assist the beginning reader. The concepts of "no," "some," and "many" are introduced. The photographs clearly illustrate the text and support the reader in making meaning from the words. Children may need assistance in using the Table of Contents, Words to Know, Read More, Internet Sites, and Index/Word List sections of the book.

Index/Word List

Word Count: 62
Early-Intervention Level: 5